Scotland's most exciting example of 21st Century engineering, The Falkirk Wheel, is more than just the World's first rotating boatlift. It is a symbol celebrating the dawn of Britain's new canal age.

The Falkirk Wheel is designed to raise or lower boats between two different height canals. Yet contrasting with this simple role is a shape that is far from conventional. In combining art and engineering, the Wheel's designers have produced a dramatic moving sculpture.

Its architecture is likened to double-headed Celtic axes, or a vast propeller symbolic of Glasgow's shipbuilding era. Yet whatever your imagination sees, The Falkirk Wheel is now firmly established as one of Scotland's most recognisable Monuments to the Future.

As the Wheel turns, water and boats - contained in its two large gondolas - are transferred between an aqueduct linked to the upper Union Canal and, 25 metres below, a basin feeding to the adjacent Forth & Clyde Canal. In so doing the boatlift reconnects, after a 70 year gap, Scotland's two leading Lowland Canals, both now rescued from decades of accelerating neglect.

In the late 1990s, British Waterways Scotland - now renamed Scottish Canals - led an ambitious scheme to restore and reopen these once proud industrial canals to create a 'corridor of opportunity' across Scotland's central belt. Known as The Millennium Link, the project once again offers not only a direct waterway route between Edinburgh and Glasgow, but also a coast to coast connection linking the rivers Forth and Clyde.

The prime aim has been to encourage new canalside investment. And, within just the first decade of reopening, the rejuvenated route has acted as a catalyst to over £400 million of retail, commercial and housing development - plus fast growing leisure facilities on and alongside both canals.

How, though, was this mammoth reconstruction scheme achieved in half the time originally planned? And how can a row of different sized cogs help turn the vast 1800 tonne Falkirk Wheel using only the same power as six kettles?

This guide provides the answers as it tells the story of a project that offers both the canal network's most exciting white knuckle ride and a new waterway designed for a new Millennium.

0 Kilometres 100
0 Miles 60
N
Atlantic Ocean
North Sea
INVERNESS
Loch Dochfour
Caledonian Canal
Loch Ness
ABERDEEN
Loch Oich
Corpach
Loch Lochy
FORT WILLIAM
SCOTLAND
Crinan Canal
Millennium Link
Forth & Clyde Canal
EDINBURGH
GLASGOW
Union Canal
Monkland Canal
THE FALKIRK WHEEL

The Millennium Link - A Corridor of Opportunity

Creation of Britain's largest, most ambitious canal restoration scheme, The Millennium Link, has involved repair or reconstruction work on many of its 500 structures - including bridges, locks and aqueducts - along the total 114km length of Scotland's two major Lowland Canals; the Union and the Forth & Clyde.

Begun in 1999, the project included sections of new canal being cut through Edinburgh's suburbs, while long buried locks were unearthed near Glasgow. New bridges have been built and original crossings refurbished.

In just three years of hectic reconstruction, rotting lock gates and stretches of long

abandoned stagnant canal - boasting little more than dumped supermarket trolleys and old tyres - have been transformed into 21st Century waterways, linked by the magnificent 35 metre high Falkirk Wheel.

The canals' 20 million annual visitors enjoy sea to sea boating facilities, with new marinas providing over 350 berths for a wide range of pleasure boats. Canoeing, kayaking and water zorbing tempt the more adventurous holiday makers, while over 100km of refurbished towpath offers unrivalled walking and cycling opportunities.

The route plays host to a wealth of varied wildlife and protected rare plants that have survived, despite - and in some cases because of - its neglected years.

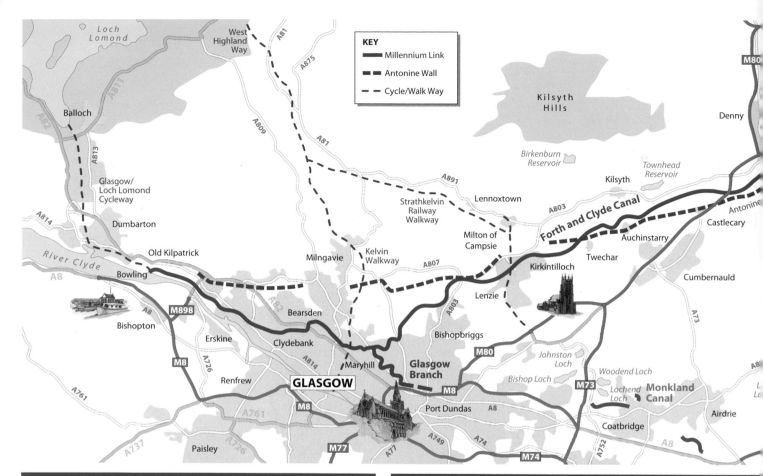

KEY
— Millennium Link
- - - Antonine Wall
- - Cycle/Walk Way

Loch Lomond

West Highland Way

Balloch

Glasgow/Loch Lomond Cycleway

Dumbarton

River Clyde

Old Kilpatrick

Bowling

Bishopton

Erskine

Renfrew

Paisley

Milngavie

Bearsden

Clydebank

Maryhill

GLASGOW

Kelvin Walkway

Strathkelvin Railway Walkway

Milton of Campsie

Lennoxtown

Kilsyth Hills

Birkenburn Reservoir

Townhead Reservoir

Kilsyth

Forth and Clyde Canal

Twechar

Kirkintilloch

Lenzie

Auchinstarry

Castlecary

Antonine

Denny

Cumbernauld

Bishopbriggs

Glasgow Branch

Port Dundas

Johnston Loch

Bishop Loch

Woodend Loch

Lochend Loch

Monkland Canal

Coatbridge

Airdrie

A Constant Water Supply

The Forth & Clyde transfers 40 million litres of water every day as its route drops 47 metres to each coastline through 20 locks either side of its highest level; known as the Summit Pound. This 30km stretch of level canal, centred on Kirkintilloch, is replenished daily with water drawn from an interconnected network of 10 reservoirs. Gauges along the canal route indicate when water levels need topping up and sluice gates are opened in the upland reservoirs.

The Union Canal is a rare 'all on one level' contour canal with no locks along its main length. It needs a lower volume of top-up water drawn from Cobbinshaw Reservoir, West Lothian.

Scotland's First Transport Corridor

The Millennium Link Project refurbished two major canals; the 61km long Forth & Clyde and the Union Canal, originally 51km. They are connected by The Falkirk Wheel where the Union Canal has been lengthened by 2km with locks and a tunnel.

Scotland's oldest canal, The Forth & Clyde - originally

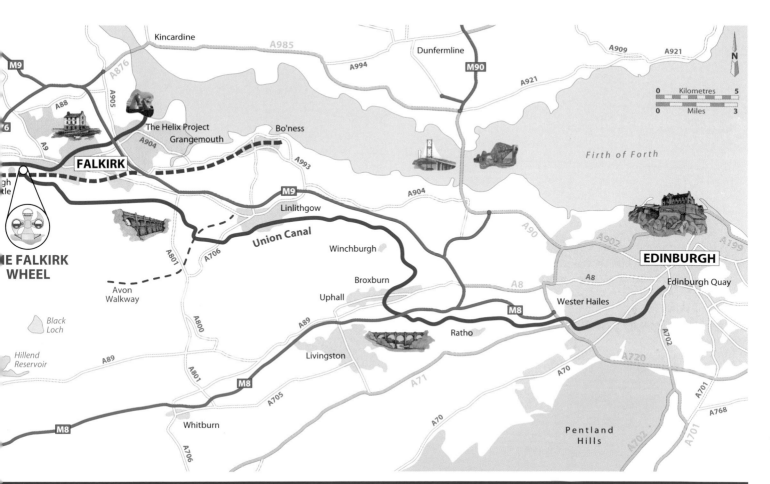

Kincardine
A985
A876
Dunfermline
M9
A994
M90
A909 A921
A88
A905
A921
The Helix Project
Grangemouth
Bo'ness
A904
A993
Firth of Forth
FALKIRK
A9
A904
M9
Linlithgow
gh
tle
THE FALKIRK
WHEEL
EDINBURGH
Union Canal
Winchburgh
A90
A902
A199
A801
A706
Broxburn
A8
Edinburgh Quay
Avon
Walkway
Uphall
A8
Wester Hailes
M8
Black
Loch
A800
A89
Ratho
A702
Hillend
Reservoir
A89
Livingston
A71
A70
A720
A801
M8
A701
A768
M8
A705
Whitburn
A70
Pentland
Hills
A702
A701
A706

0   Kilometres   5
0   Miles   3

N

known as The Great Canal - runs 57km coast to coast between the ports of Bowling on the Clyde and Grangemouth on the Firth of Forth, with a 4km spur into Glasgow. The link between Grangemouth and Glasgow was completed in 1777, offering the city a direct connection to the North Sea and opening up trade with the Baltic, Scandinavia and Holland. The route from Glasgow, west to the Clyde, opened 13 years later.

The 1822 Union Canal has no locks along its main length. Known as a contour canal, it was built by engineer Hugh Baird all on one level - and to the incredible accuracy of just 25mm - along the 73.1 metre contour line. Its barges carried a wide range of products into and out of the very heart of Edinburgh.

Boats and barges navigating the lower Forth & Clyde were raised 34 metres up to the

Union by a flight of 11 locks linking the two canals at Camelon, near Falkirk.

The Forth & Clyde closed to through navigation in 1963 when the A80 Glasgow to Stirling road was routed at low level across the canal at Castlecary.

The Union suffered a similar fate two years later, severed by the new M8 motorway west of Edinburgh.

cotland's earliest canal, The Forth & Clyde, was completed in 1790 and quickly became established as a major transport route, providing a vital artery for the development of the central belt.

   As also the World's first sea to sea ship canal, its tall-masted ships demanded bridges that swung or lifted open as cargoes, including sugar, timber and grain, sailed through 40 locks, right across Scotland to and from Baltic ports. A major shipping centre rapidly became established at Port Dundas in the centre of Glasgow, with a wealth of goods - including whisky from the Western Isles - featured on the trading manifests.

Scotland's famous West Coast puffers, many built in the canal's own half dozen inland boatyards, became a common sight ferrying their cargoes between the central belt and outer islands.

The canal also opened up regular commercial services to far flung places like Hamburg, St. Petersburg and Trieste. Beside its towpath new industries, such as boat building, munitions factories, brickworks and distilleries, soon flourished.

The shorter Union Canal opened 32 years later towards the end of the canal building era. The route was cut all on one level with no locks along its main length. Horse-pulled barges ferried coal, stone and even manure beneath fixed arch bridges, and across spectacular aqueducts, to the city homes, factories and farms of 19th Century Edinburgh.

With roads just rough tracks, and railways still being developed, these busy waterways were the motorways of their age - the country's first commercial transport network.

By the 1830s up to 200,000 passengers travelled the route annually. Daytrippers 'took the air' journeying on pleasure steamers, and a considerable proportion of the route's annual three million tonnes of cargo was transported the full distance between Scotland's main conurbations, Glasgow and Edinburgh, via the flight of 11 locks linking the two canals near Falkirk.

Despite waterborne trade being hit by the arrival of the railways in the 1840s, both canals flourished until the First World War when Grangemouth docks, the route's important eastern sea link into the Firth of Forth, was closed as a security measure. The canals' role as transport corridors rapidly

STRANGE BUT TRUE

Slimline 'swiftboats', pulled by the fastest horses and carrying 60 passengers, operated a seven hour express service between Glasgow and Edinburgh. A scythe, projecting from the boat's prow, would cut through the tow line of any slow moving vessels which failed to give way. At Falkirk's flight of locks, passengers saved time by changing boats.

EDINBURGH
AND
GLASGOW.

THE FORTH & CLYDE
AND UNION CANAL
PASSAGE BOAT,
SWIFT.

Until the SECOND LIGHT PASSAGE BOAT now building at Tophill, near Port-Downie is finished, the SWIFT will sail as follows:—

FROM
Port-Dundas, Glasgow,
Every MONDAY, WEDNESDAY, & FRIDAY,
At half-past Seven o'Clock Morning.

FROM
Port-Hopetoun, Edinburgh,
Every TUESDAY, THURSDAY, & SATURDAY,
At Eight o'Clock Morning.

Canal Office, Port-Dundas,
GLASGOW, 10th November, 1830.

Aitken & Co. Printers.

Courtesy Falkirk Museums

declined, taken over by the now fast growing railway network.

The axe fell in the 1960s when new roads and motorways were built across both canals at low level, brutally severing them as navigation routes. The future use of a limited headroom Forth & Clyde, with its sea going vessels, was not foreseen. So, in 1963, the A80 road at Castlecary was routed across the canal by constructing a low embankment instead of incorporating a more expensive bridge option.

A similar decision a couple of years later, involving the M8 motorway into Edinburgh, killed through navigation on the Union Canal.

For decades the canals lay virtually abandoned, maintained only for safety and to allow their role as vital land drains to continue. Bridges were filled in, crumbling lock gates let the water through without the need for lock keepers. The waterways seemed forgotten.

STRANGE BUT TRUE

*K*eystones on the Union Canal's Laughin' and Greetin' Bridge are carved with a laughing face on one side and a sad one on the other. This reflects the successful builder who cut an easy stretch of canal one side of the bridge, and the unfortunate one who nearly went bankrupt digging a tunnel on the other side.

The Race to Refurbish

When engineers arrived in 1999 to refurbish the two derelict canals, they were met by a route obstructed in 32 places by infilled bridges or pipelines; all of which had to be removed. Most of the locks, bridges and aqueducts needed at least some repair work and the challenges of raising all the finance meant refurbishment started two years late.

Original completion dates, on which much of the funding depended, had though still to be met; so the intended five year rescue programme had to be cut to three. Planning and programming this restoration work, without affecting the canals' vital role as drainage channels, proved a significant logistical exercise.

At Wester Hailes in Edinburgh, a new 1.7km length of the Union Canal had to be cut as the original route had long since been infilled. In Glasgow's suburbs, three buried Forth & Clyde locks were unearthed and restored, while eight new ones have been built near Falkirk.

11

The Environmental Artery – So Much to See For Free

Stretching coast to coast, and invading the catchments of both the rivers Forth and Clyde, the canals act as an important environmental corridor, rich in wildlife and aquatic plants. The overall route, though a relatively small wetland area compared to Scotland's many rivers and lochs, offers a unique combination of shallow, stable, slow flowing and nutrient rich water, well aerated as it falls over numerous lock gates.

The canals form vital links between isolated wildlife areas and support an impressive range of wetland plants, invertebrates, amphibians, birds and mammals. The result is a rare combination of over 300 plant species, and the animals that depend on them. The creation of several nature conservation sites along or near the canals is recognition of their wildlife value.

The water is home to over 30 varieties of aquatic plants; 15 species of mollusc; 33 different types of water flea and even freshwater sponges. Invertebrates, sporting such intriguing names as the 'wandering snail' or 'greater ramshorn', inhabit the canal bed.

Pike, roach, perch, eels and even brown trout share the water with mallard, coots and, curiously, red-eared terrapins sporting an up to 100 year lifespan and thought to be long abandoned pets.

Lurking in bankside vegetation are 'lesser water boatmen' and beetles of every variety except Liverpudlian singers. Many of the plants near the canal edge, like the stress-relieving valerian, were used as herbal remedies long before the days of the National Health Service.

Rare and protected plants include Bennett's pondweed, Tufted Loosestrife and Royal Fern. Otters, bats, mink, water voles and roe deer have all been sighted and mute swans regularly nest alongside the canal.

To explore this wildlife corridor, £4 million has been invested in creating more than 100km of generally 'soft' towpath. Used by over 20 million walkers, joggers, tourists and cyclists every year, these towpaths offer a refreshing breadth of fresh air, contributing to the impressive health-enhancing claims of these now leisure-orientated waterways.

Independent analysis of the additional physical activity generated by the canal environment estimates an impressive £6.4 million annual saving on the region's total health bill.

Schoolchildren are also major beneficiaries of Scotland's busiest cross-country paths. The Millennium Link regularly plays host to educational nature walks, boat trips and workshops, all now recognised aspects of Scottish schools 'curriculum for excellence'.

The mid 1970s saw renewed interest - led mainly by the voluntary sector and canal enthusiasts - in the use of water routes; this time for leisure activities. British Waterways began to realise its liabilities could be turned into assets, as catalysts encouraging canalside development, and gradually the tide started turning.

In Scotland, two initiatives - the Glasgow and the West Lothian Canal Projects - were completed during the 1990s, refurbishing sections of canal and removing four obstructions to navigation along the route.

The arrival in 1994 of the lottery-funded Millennium Commission opened up even further opportunities. Scottish Enterprise, European agencies and local councils all rallied round to help raise the finance needed for British Waterways Scotland's pioneering scheme to revitalise the full length of the two canals.

Public support was high. When the project was threatened with cancellation, volunteers collected over 30,000 signatures petitioning for it to be given the go ahead. Yet the task of raising the required £84.5 million still proved challenging and, by the time funds were finally on the table, a planned five year reconstruction programme had to be achieved in only three.

At construction sites across Scotland an army of 700 modernday 'navvies' - the description used for the original builders of 'navigable' waterways - constructed new timber lock gates and abseiled down the sides of aqueducts to return a route, all of

15

which by then was a Scheduled Monument, back to its former glory.

When Her Majesty the Queen officially opened The Millennium Link in May 2002, the first seeds of canalside redevelopment were already bearing fruit.

Within a decade over £400 million of investment across the canal corridor, by both the public and private sectors, had translated into 2000 new waterside homes plus 100,000 square metres of retail and commercial development.

And, crucially for a route passing through many of Scotland's most deprived areas, some 4000 much needed jobs had been

 created. The nationwide value of this unique canal restoration scheme, originally dubbed 'The People's Project', is undisputedly proving its worth.

The Forth & Clyde Canal

- The World's first sea to sea ship canal.
- 61km long, with 38 operating locks, 38 bridges and 25 aqueducts.
- Built 1768 - 1790 by engineers John Smeaton and Robert Whitworth.

The Union Canal

- A rare contour canal all excavated to the same level.
- Built 1818-1822 by engineer Hugh Baird.
- Originally 51km long with 84 bridges - 62 of them arch bridges - 24 aqueducts, Scotland's only canal tunnel, but no locks (though the flight of 11 at Falkirk was officially still on the Union Canal).
- Completion of The Falkirk Wheel site in 2002 extended the Union Canal by 2km and added three locks, two more bridges, two aqueducts, another canal tunnel and the Wheel itself.

A Catalyst for Investment

Just minutes from the heart of Edinburgh, a once abandoned large pool of stagnant water, surrounded by a wasteland of derelict factories and warehousing, has been transformed into a thriving award-winning canalside development offering its several million annual visitors shops, restaurants, pubs and offices. A popular summertime waterborne festival features music, raft races and fireworks.

This now bustling 70 berth Edinburgh Quay, forming the eastern terminus of the Union Canal, epitomises the impressive commercial achievements possible through joint ventures between Scottish Canals and entrepreneurial private sector developers.

Land either side of the canals has been opened up to create mooring berths and waterside attractions; such as the marinas at Kirkintilloch and Auchinstarry and Clydebank's exciting new waterfront shopping centre.

On and alongside the Forth & Clyde through Northern Glasgow, a vibrant new canal hub is host to the city's cultural quarter boasting major theatre, opera, drama and music activities. Rejuvenation of 400 hectares of land around nearby Speirs Wharf and Maryhill Locks has attracted new housing, offices and shops; with the area's links to the city centre enhanced by the instant 'growth' of 52 towering artificial flowers sporting two metre wide aluminium petals.

Numerous boat hire companies now offer the canals' over 20 million annual visitors a 114km length of waterway to explore;

with navigation of dramatic aqueducts, 44 teamwork-demanding locks, plus an unforgettable ride on The Falkirk Wheel, all part of the holiday experience.

A range of annual canal festivals - featuring activities as varied as dragon boat racing, street theatre and water polo - further boosts both the local economy and the enjoyment of the waterways.

The Falkirk Wheel - the making of a landmark

The Falkirk Wheel is unique. Not only is it the first boatlift of its type anywhere, but its combination of engineering ingenuity and architectural imagination creates both an eye-catching working sculpture and Scotland's most unusual tourist attraction.

During the structure's five year design period the boatlift developed from a seesaw style lift, based on ancient Greek technology, to a circular turning wheel. The end result, today's dramatic 21st Century shape, is surely the most appropriate way to celebrate Britain's new canal era.

The Wheel has already claimed its place as a major Scottish landmark and is one of the World's most important canal structures enjoyed by over 500,000 visitors every year.

The way its computer controlled motors gracefully raise or lower 500 tonnes of boats and water, contained in two large gondolas,

the 25 metre difference between two canals appears complex; but is deceptively simple.

As you journey through a canal tunnel and across an aqueduct - before seeming to drop off the end as your boat is lowered by the Wheel - you will be enjoying the most memorable yet gentle white knuckle ride.

To route both the Union Canal, and the Forth & Clyde 35 metres below it, into the Wheel site involved cutting a new canal section, building three locks and excavating Britain's first new canal tunnel for over 100 years.

A 2km extension of the Union Canal ends in a double staircase lock which lowers boats seven metres to a holding basin. From here they enter a 168 metre long canal tunnel driven beneath the Roman Antonine Wall.

Boats emerge to cross a 104 metre long aqueduct which runs directly into the Wheel's upper gondola. With up to four boats sealed into the gondola behind a pair of flap gates, the Wheel's travel time, down to a dry well alongside the lower basin, takes about five minutes.

Similar gates then release the boats into the basin from where, through a single lock, they drop three metres to join the Forth & Clyde Canal.

Hidden in a wood near Falkirk are the remains of an old, half buried canal lock. This is all that is visible of the Wheel's predecessor - a flight of 11 locks, the rest of which lie, long forgotten, beneath nearby streets.

Until 1933, this impressive group of locks linked the Union Canal with the Forth & Clyde Canal, 34 metres below and all but a day's heavy work away opening and closing some 44 lock gates.

Following the locks' closure, the two canals continued - separately - a spiral of decline and virtual abandonment. Their revival, early in 2002, as part of The Millennium Link Project, had demanded a new connection.

In 1994, Dundee-based architect Nicoll Russell Studios was asked to develop, along with British Waterways, fresh and exciting ideas worthy of a structure that was recognised from the outset as having the potential to become an international landmark. The site chosen was a steep sloping field on the outskirts of Falkirk, home of a redundant sprawling tarworks some 3km from where the original locks lie buried.

But what form of structure should be built?

The first conceptual design was based on the Greek Noria machine - a giant tipping lift used to irrigate fields. This later evolved into an open cylindrical drum containing rotating gondolas to carry the boats.

BURIED LOCKS

It took virtually a full day for boats and their owners to negotiate the Wheel's predecessor - a flight of 11 locks, abandoned in 1933 and now buried beneath Falkirk streets. Descending the 34 metre drop between the two canals used up 3500 tonnes of water every trip, and reservoirs were needed beside the locks to replenish supplies.

By contrast, The Falkirk Wheel uses no water and the same journey takes 15 minutes.

The Boatlift's Development -
From Tilting Tanks to a Rotating Wheel

Early ideas for connecting the canals ranged from a vast spoon-shaped seesaw to a funicular railway. Also among the doodles on designers' notepads were a vertical lift concealed within a cylindrical waterfall, plus turning counterweighted arms or hefty cranes raising and lowering the boats.

During the five year design stage, the concept of a turning wheel was developed, first as an open cylindrical drum. This later became a 19th Century style ferris wheel with four hanging gondolas. The appreciation that a wheel does not also demand a rim, led to today's striking design.

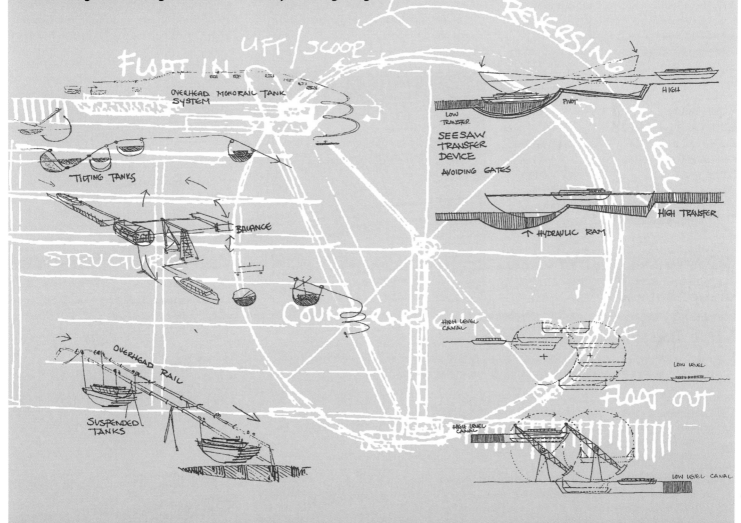

By 1999, the challenges of making this difficult concept workable had led to a fairground style ferris wheel design with four hanging, rather than rotating, gondolas. This was the shape originally intended to be built.

However, with a construction company chosen, British Waterways felt that this somewhat clumsy looking design could be improved to create a more modern structure worthy of celebrating a new Millennium. A hectic month of meetings followed as a 20 strong team of engineers, architects and steelwork fabricators brainstormed their way through yet more ideas.

The result has won major design awards worldwide. Yet there are virtually as many ways to describe what its shape represents as there are people asked.

The Falkirk Wheel

- The World's first rotating boatlift, 35 metres high and 27 metres long. The total project cost £20 million to build and was opened in 2002.

- The Wheel weighs 1200 tonnes, plus two 50 tonne gondolas. Each gondola transfers a total 250 tonnes of boats and water the 25 metre vertical distance between the Union and Forth & Clyde Canals.

- Boat journeys through the Wheel take 15 minutes overall; but the gondolas complete their half turn between the two canal heights in just five minutes.

THE FALKIRK WHEEL

Precision Engineering - Big Scale

Although centre stage, the 1800 tonne Wheel costs about quarter of the overall £20 million price tag for The Falkirk Wheel complex with its aqueduct, tunnel, canal extension and locks.

Main components of the Wheel were trial assembled at steel fabricator, Butterley Engineering's, Derbyshire factory to check everything fitted, and then bolted together again on site prior to lifting into position.

This attention to detail meant that the planned week long erection operation was completed a day early. Components were generally positioned to an accuracy of 10mm, with the 25 metre long axle section aligned to just 1mm.

As the Wheel turns, stresses imposed on the structure by the total 600 tonne weight of water-filled gondolas change completely in direction. Instead of using normal welded joints, steel sections were bolted together, making them more robust to resist fatigue induced stresses.

This gave the construction team the awesome task of mating 15,000 bolts with over 45,000 bolt holes.

Falkirk Wheel Construction Team

Client:	British Waterways Scotland - now renamed Scottish Canals
Conceptual design:	Nicoll Russell Studios/British Waterways Scotland
Main contractor:	Morrison Construction - Bachy Soletanche Joint Venture
Steelwork:	Butterley Engineering
Architect:	RMJM
Designers:	
Civil engineering;	Arup Consultants/Tony Gee & Partners
Mechanical engineering;	Bennett Associates
Control systems:	Fairfield Controls

How the Wheel Works

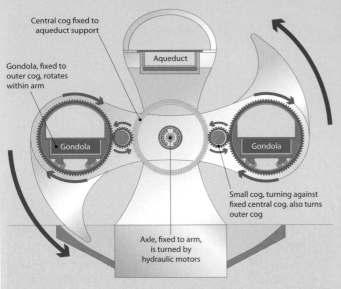

Central cog fixed to aqueduct support

Aqueduct

Gondola, fixed to outer cog, rotates within arm

Gondola

Gondola

Small cog, turning against fixed central cog. also turns outer cog

Axle, fixed to arm, is turned by hydraulic motors

Turning the Wheel involves two simple engineering functions that have been brought together to create an innovative, energy saving combination.

The prime mechanism is a series of hydraulic motors that rotate the four metre diameter central axle and the Wheel's two propeller-shaped arms fixed to it. Helping to keep the gondolas, and the boats inside them, horizontal throughout the operation is the second mechanism - a row of linked cogs that interact as the Wheel turns, but need no power supply.

The 10 hydraulic motors are positioned around a fixed plate behind the axle. As an outer ring of teeth on each motor rotates, it engages with similar teeth on the axle rim, turning the axle and, with it, the entire Wheel.

One half revolution, moving boats between the two canals, takes less then five minutes. Though, with boats loading and unloading, total journey time is around 15 minutes.

As both 50 tonne gondolas contain the same 250 tonne weight of water and boats, the perfectly balanced Wheel needs only 1.5kW hours of electricity - costing just a few pence - to complete a half turn. The really clever bit though is ensuring that the 25 metre long gondolas - supported at each end inside circular holes in the main propeller arms - always remain horizontal.

As the arms turn, bogie wheels, fixed beneath the ends of each gondola, run around a single curved rail attached to the inside rim of the hole in each arm. In theory this should be sufficient to keep the gondolas level. But wheel friction in the bogies, or any sudden movement of so much water, could result in a gondola sticking or tilting.

To ensure this could never happen, and water and boats always remain level throughout the turning cycle, a row of linked cogs acts as a fail-safe backup. One end of each gondola is fixed to the large outside cogs in this row of five, which is hidden behind the inside arm.

These outer eight metre diameter cogs are exactly the same size as the central one in the row, which is attached to the aqueduct's support column and cannot turn. Two smaller cogs, attached to the arm, lie between these larger ones to link all five.

When the Wheel rotates, these small cogs move with it and their toothed edges turn against both the fixed central cog and the outer ones to which the gondolas are joined. With these large cogs all the same size, the attached gondolas rotate at the exact same speed as the Wheel - but in the opposite direction. In other words, the gondolas are always horizontal no matter where the Wheel is in its cycle.

Simple, safe, innovative and energy free.

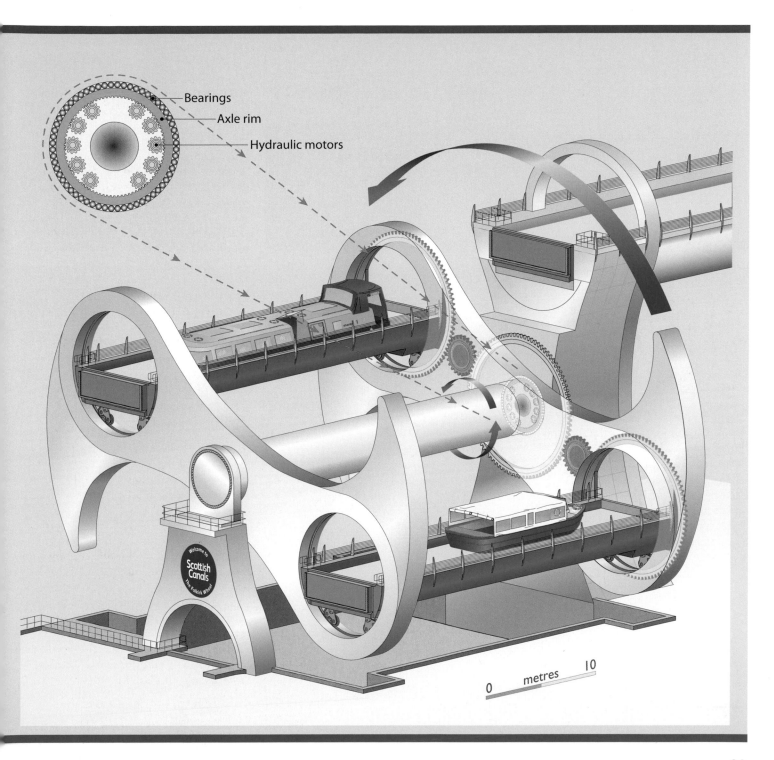

Bearings

Axle rim

Hydraulic motors

Welcome to
Scottish
Canals
The Falkirk Wheel

0   metres   10

Most images encompass Scottish or marine architectural themes. But take your pick from; Celtic inspired double-headed axes, the spine of a fish, ribcage of a whale, or the vast turning propellers of a Clyde built ship.

The Wheel itself lies at the end of a reinforced concrete aqueduct which is linked, via a tunnel and a double staircase lock, to the Union Canal. Boats entering the Wheel's upper gondola are lowered, along with the water they float in, to the basin below. At the same time an equal weight of boats and water rises up in the other gondola.

A row of five cogs ensures the gondolas always remain horizontal. The balanced Wheel is turned so efficiently by hydraulic motors, that the electricity cost needed for one half revolution is just a few pence.

Everything is computer controlled - even water levels in the aqueduct and lower basin - but the Wheel's mechanics involve only proven, fail safe engineering. It is the way this technology has been cleverly combined into one structure that makes The Falkirk Wheel unique.

The secret to the boatlift's smooth, economic operation is ensuring that both loaded gondolas weigh virtually the same, so that the Wheel remains balanced. Archimedes Principle guarantees that, as a boat enters the gondola, it displaces exactly its own weight in water. So, regardless of whether gondolas are empty or full of boats, they will be carrying the same load.

The only variable able to create an imbalance is differing water depths and it is

essential gondolas contain very nearly the same level of water. This is dependent on water levels in both the aqueduct leading to the Wheel and in the lower basin. These water levels are also influenced by locks at the site's entry and exit points above and below the Wheel.

Water levels throughout the complex are monitored and controlled around the clock by an extensive network of sensors, valves and hidden bypass pipes. State of the art computer software records water depth to a few millimetres, and allows only a maximum

75mm difference between levels in each gondola. The computers can even predict if tolerances are likely to be exceeded and take early preventative action.

With water levels balanced, steel gates at both ends of the gondolas, and where they dock with the aqueduct and lower basin, tilt open or shut. As a gondola arrives, a rubber seal springs out across the bottom and sides of the 50mm wide air gap between it and either the aqueduct or lower basin.

Water is pumped into the much larger gap between the end gates on either structure, ensuring levels remain equal, before both gates fold down flat to allow boats in or out. The sequence is then reversed, with the two gates rotating up to the vertical again. The gap between them is pumped dry and the rubber seal retracted hydraulically. This allows the gondola to be raised or lowered as the Wheel turns.

As boats leave the upper gondola they enter a 104 metre long concrete aqueduct. With its trough passing through circular hoops, this heavy structure created challenges for its designers.

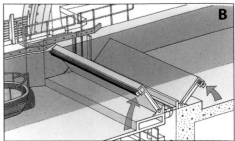
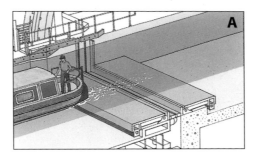
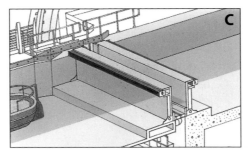
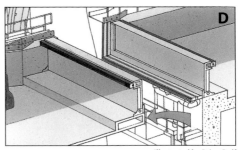

Illustrated by Brian Delf

The Romans Were Here First

The Wheel shares its site with another important engineering structure that pre-dates it by over 1800 years. A short, well marked, walk from the Wheel takes visitors to fields and woodland containing the remains of the Roman Antonine Wall and one of its defensive forts, Rough Castle.

Designated a UNESCO World Heritage site, little now remains of the four metre high wall, though the deep, up to 12 metre wide ditch on its northern flank is still visible.

Built of turf laid over broad cobbled foundations, the wall had a wooden walkway along the top. It once marked the northern frontier of a Roman Empire that stretched 5000km from Britain's Atlantic coast east across Europe, the Middle East and Africa to Morocco.

The wall had been ordered by Emperor Antonius Pius around AD 142 and this section is the best preserved in its entire 60km length from Bo'ness on the River Forth west to Old Kilpatrick on the Clyde.

Similarly, Rough Castle alongside it is among the most recognisable of an original 19 forts built along the route to defend the wall's southern flank. Again only a complex of ditches and mounds now defines where, some 1870 years ago, stone and timber buildings housed the fort's 450 strong infantry garrison. The soldiers' role was to defend the frontier from northern Celtic tribes and to collect taxes from the Roman Empire's subjects.

The wall and fort remained in use for only 20 years before the Romans withdrew south to the more substantial stone frontier, Hadrian's Wall in what is now Northumberland. The structure was though not totally forgotten as 18th Century navvies, cutting the Forth & Clyde Canal, reused sections of the old wall's ditch for their route.

Today's most eagle-eyed visitors should be able to find a patchwork of odd looking circular indents in the fields around the site. These are the remains of deep pits called lilia, once the fort's most gruesome secret defence. With each pit containing a sharpened stake concealed by brushwood, attackers falling in suffered a painful end.

Celtic Water Horses to Guard the Canal

While visiting the Wheel, why not take a pleasant 6km walk or boat ride east along the Forth & Clyde Canal to view another of the region's iconic modernday sculptures depicting vast shimmering horses' heads.

Beside the canal, on the site of a new 350 hectare urban park bordering Falkirk, stand two 30 metre high steel-plated sculptures resembling mythical Celtic water horses called Kelpies.

Such imaginary creatures, rumoured to once frequent Scotland's lochs and rivers, could also be thought of as a reminder of the last canal era's working towpath horses. Or they could be the reincarnation of reputedly the World's largest horse - a 1930s Clydesdale which delivered wagon loads of Scotland's famous soft drink Irn-Bru around the streets of nearby Falkirk.

The twin hollow heads, each intricately formed of 500 separate squares of steel plate to create a semi-translucent skin, tower either side of a new lock. Along with a marina and canal extension, the lock provides a dramatic gateway into the Forth & Clyde from the River Carron.

These impressive sculptures form a focal point of the surrounding Helix eco park itself boasting wide ranging pleasure activities. A large lagoon offers water attractions as divergent as sailing and water polo. A nearby events arena features pop concerts while, within extensive woodland, deer, sparrow hawks and owls could be sighted.

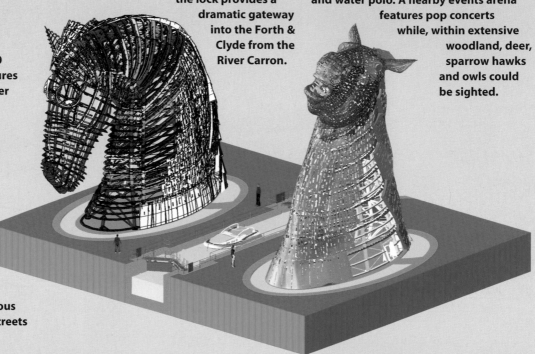

Note how the trough is connected only at two points around the hoops and imagine the high structural forces passing through this small area of concrete, which needs to be heavily reinforced with numerous steel bars. The upper half of each hoop is hollow, made not of concrete but lightweight glass reinforced plastic.

Leaving the aqueduct, boats enter Britain's first new canal tunnel to be built for over a century. Here visitors sail beneath the remains of the Roman Antonine Wall.

No ground disturbance was allowed near the remains of this historic earth wall, so the 168 metre tunnel was excavated very carefully in three stages. The tunnel floor is formed of thick reinforced concrete to support it over old fireclay mine workings beneath.

Dates

1768-1790: Forth & Clyde Canal built

1818-1822: Union Canal built

1933: Falkirk Locks closed and built over

1963: Forth & Clyde Canal closed to through navigation

1965: Union Canal similarly closed.

1999-2001: Both canals refurbished creating The Millennium Link

2000-2002: The Falkirk Wheel built

2002: The Millennium Link and Falkirk Wheel opened by Her Majesty The Queen

2012: The Wheel celebrates its tenth birthday in the presence of Her Royal Highness Princess Anne

2012-2013: Development of Helix Urban Park and Kelpies Water Horse sculptures

Unlocking Scotland's Potential

The impressive first decade success of the Millennium Link, with The Falkirk Wheel at its centre, has already exceeded the expectations of those entrepreneurial canal enthusiasts, within voluntary groups and what was then British Waterways Scotland, who conceived the vision in the 1990s.

Over the next decade the rejuvenated route is expected to more than quadruple to 16,000 the jobs it has already created. Today's 2000 new canalside homes will spiral to an estimated 14,000 with total inward investment along the route by 2020 predicted to be around £2 billion.

At either end of the canals, Scotland's two principal cities - Edinburgh and Glasgow - could soon offer floating 21st Century homes in their new marinas. Locks may be powered by mini hydro electric schemes or wind turbines.

The existing maze of fibre optic cabling beneath towpaths could grow exponentially and innovative surface water drainage schemes, feeding into the canals, increase the sustainability of waterside developments.

The country's Lowland Canals have survived battles against the railways, low level road crossings, supermarket trolleys and decades of abandonment.

This once 19th Century route for coal barges and cargo-laden sailing ships is now even more comfortable with its 21st Century traffic of colourful canal boats, canoes and sea going yachts. And it boasts - in The Falkirk Wheel - one of the country's top tourist attractions.

This 'ribbon of opportunity' is undeniably a win-win project as it continues to unlock Scotland's potential.